Whet

Tanya Salter

Copyright © 2022 Tanya Salter

All rights reserved.

ISBN: 9781729145166

DEDICATION

This book is dedicated to all who desire more of God's Word. To those who do not hold a seminary degree, but thirst for more.

CONTENTS

ACKNOWLEDGMENTS

Jesse McCoskey and Jimmie Sue Primmer were encouraging when I provided devotions via the internet for a season while at FBC Scottsmoor.

JoAnne LaFont, who found ways to encourage me when we attended different churches. It meant a lot knowing that she thought the work had value.

Jim Johnson with Just a Preacher Ministries who took the time to read one of my earlier manuscripts and encouraged me that my writing was sound.

Brother Greg Parsley at Calvary Baptist Church of Grant, Florida, who kept insisting that I needed to get some of these devotionals published. He never missed an opportunity to encourage and ask me how it was coming along.

My pastors who are gifted in bringing the Scriptures to life, which enabled me to grow as a Christian. Some of them are Dennis Chapman, Dave Anderson, Gary Bullard, Dan Reaves, Terry Jones, Larry Bazer, and Scott Wilson.

Thanks to my family who over the past ten years listened to my ramblings, critiqued the devotionals. Without them this book of devotions would not have come to fruition. Thank you for believing in me when I did not believe in myself.

CHAPTER 1: DEVOTIONS 1-7

Devotion 1: O Taste and See

Passage: Psalm 34
Key Verse: Psalm 34:8

Take a trip with me down memory lane and think of a holiday where the food was overflowing and in abundance. Maybe it was a holiday like the 4th of July or Thanksgiving, or perhaps it was a birthday, a potluck at church, or maybe it was even a wedding celebration. This means the food had been cooked, was abundant, on display, and waiting for the first ones to sink their teeth into its lush offerings. It is during these times that I cannot help but think about the words of Psalm 34:8. Go ahead and look up the verse, read it, and let the words penetrate for a moment.

Around special occasions our eyes behold the buffet table and many of us are ready to sink our fork into that apple pie, triple chocolate brownie, or maybe even that green bean casserole. As we contemplate what to actually indulge in (let's face it most of us do not have self-control), can we truly say "The Lord is good"? Better yet, can we say with the psalmist "O taste and see that the Lord is good"?

The second statement unlike the first, implies that you have some experience with the Lord, that you have experienced tasting and seeing the Lord. Tasting is not something you can do just by casually looking at the buffet table. Have you intently stared at the fluffy mashed potatoes and smelled the aroma of the apple pie? Did you sink your teeth into the green bean casserole or devour the salad? Did your hands feel the warm rolls or cool glass of beverage? Did you smother gravy all over your food? Did you have an opportunity to slice your meat or pierce that okra? When we enjoy a meal often times, we use all our senses, not just our taste buds to take the experience to the next level.

The same can be said of our walk with Christ. Can you say you have actively experienced Him and His word, not just passively glanced over both? Have we as a group of Christ followers intently with all our senses engaged, truly found the Lord to be good? Let us together, taste and see that the Lord is good!

Devotion 2: Permission Requested
Passage: Mark 5:1-20
Key Verse: Mark 5:12

Please take a look at Mark 5:1–20, it is a very exciting piece of New Testament Scripture. This passage reminds me of the Old Testament record of Job. If you remember in the book of Job (Job 1:7-12; 2:3-6), Satan requested permission from God to try to get Job to curse God. God granted permission to Satan to cause the huge, heavy, draining heartache for Job that would last his whole life (just ask anyone who has had to mourn the death of a child, much less mourn the death of all their children!).

Similarly, in Mark 5 we see the demons asking Jesus for permission to enter the herd of swine (pigs) when they leave the demoniac. Jesus granted their request (Mark 5:12–13a). Did you notice that we have examples in both the Old *and* New Testaments of Satan asking permission of our Lord? Satan does not have permission to do anything he wishes to do!

What does this mean for the Christian? Simply put, it means that the evil and demonic world moves against Christians with the permission of our Lord. You can rest assured that *nothing* happens to you that God does not know about. Yes, bad things might happen, but God is in there to guide, support, and light the way for us. Thanks to Job's experience many of us can quote Job 1:21 in times of trials. Look it up if you do not know the verse.

Thanks to the demon-possessed man in Mark 5, we know that when we seek God the demons do flee, and that *the evil spirit world does not run around doing whatever it pleases, going wherever it wants to go.* Imagine if we understood that principle in an active, intentional way. How it **would** change the way we walk…no longer would we walk in fear. Does this make you hunger to discover more truths located throughout God's love letter to us? I know it makes me want to know more, stumble upon more, intentionally search for more in the Scriptures because He is good.

Devotion 3: Second Chances
Passage: Jonah
Key Verse: Jonah 3:1

If you and I were ever to meet one another in the future, one thing you would quickly learn about me, is that I am hearing impaired. During our conversation I might say things like "huh?", "who?", and "what's that?" Sometimes it gets annoying, *even* for me. Yet, I am reminded of our Heavenly Father, who repeats things for us. Take some time to read the small book of Jonah (especially if you are not familiar with the life of Jonah); it is only 4 chapters long and short ones at that.

Have you ever heard God speak and then *intentionally* decide to ignore Him and not do what He asked you to do? This is precisely where Jonah found himself. Jonah had decided not to go to Nineveh as God had asked (Jonah 1:2). Then, after a once-in-a-lifetime smelly event, Jonah gets vomited up by a great fish and God speaks *again*.

God gave Jonah instructions a *second time* to go to Nineveh and preach what he is told to preach (Jonah 3:1–2). While God is not obligated to give us a second chance, why not answer "Yes, Lord" if He does? Now, that is something to get your appetite going! He does not throw you out just because you did not listen the first time. I heard Dave Ramsey say basically: "God is not mad at you, He misses you." Wouldn't you like to know the God who is so crazy about you that He sometimes repeats His instructions to you? O taste and see that the Lord is good.

Devotion 4: Confidence Grower
Passage: Exodus 3-4
Key Verse: Exodus 3:12

Ever complete a task or a job that made you stand a little taller or give you a little confidence? Did the completion of that task make you ready to take on another? Did the completion of that task make you feel good, satisfied, or even proud of what you accomplished? I have been there. It is a feeling of complete and total satisfaction not of arrogance, that you have arrived.

I am continually amazed at the way God addresses Moses's lack of trust in Him and in himself (Moses). You can see zero confidence in Moses over the task that was presented to him to do (Exodus 3:11). Carefully, slowly, and intentionally read Exodus 3:12.

Did you catch it? God tells Moses that he would know that God sent him *after* the job was completed (not before it started and not while he did the job). Now, let that sink in for a moment and then reread verse 12.

Interestingly, the few signs that God would show Moses were for the sake of others to believe (Exodus 4:1–5, 6–8) *not* for Moses to believe. God gave Moses God's name ("I Am"), the changing rod, and the leprous hand that was made well, all for the benefit of *others* and not for the faith of Moses. In this historical account found in the Scriptures, the signs were given for the building of others' faith, not for the person with whom God was immediately speaking with.

Tokens are for remembrances. Moses would look back on a *completed* job and know that it was God who sent him to do the job. A completed job, in this instance not the assignment of the job, nor the working of the job, is what would give Moses the confidence booster. The Lord does and will grow confidence through completed tasks. What tasks have you completed that grew your faith? What tasks were bigger than you that God completed through you? Finish the task and see your faith grow! O taste and see that the Lord is good…go ahead do what He has asked you to do and watch your confidence and faith grow.

Devotion 5: Distress

Passage: Psalm 120
Key Verse: Psalm 120:1

As I grow in my Christian walk, I understand more of what the Psalmist was articulating in Psalm 120:1. While being in distress certainly is no fun, it gives us an opportunity to learn to cry out to our Lord. Have you ever experienced a time when you were hurting emotionally, and *no one* was around? Or worse yet, others were around but you could not bring yourself to let them know you were hurting? Maybe it was the death of a loved one or a relationship. Possibly, it was when you received a rejection letter from a college, potential employer, or even from a loved one. It is the place that none of us wants to find ourselves, but it is the very place where we can learn an important Spiritual discipline. If you have not read Psalm 120:1, now would be a good time, prior to going any further in this reading.

When we are in distress, the spiritual practice of crying out comes with a benefit and it is a *huge* one. Many of us erroneously believe we are "self-made", and we do not bring ourselves to the humble position of crying out to God. Yes, we might cry out to a friend, or a family member eventually, or even post it all over Facebook and other social media outlets, but it usually takes us a while to cry out to God (if ever).

When we finally cry out to the Lord, He *hears* us. To me nothing is worse than being all alone and uncared for during times of distress. We are not beyond the hearing of God, and if not beyond His hearing, then we certainly are not alone. Distress and loneliness tell us big ol' bold lies that we are indeed alone and that no one cares. The truth however, is that our heavenly Father loves us so. O taste and see that the Lord is good, and that He hears us when we cry out to Him in our distress. Therefore; *we can know we are not alone* in our distress today or ever, regardless of where we are or what situation we find ourselves in.

Devotion 6: Repentance
Passage: Matthew 4:12-22
Key Verse: Matthew 4:17

I hear more and more "What is the big deal about repentance? Everyone makes mistakes". Rarely do I hear, "Everyone sins and needs to do something about it." We have become almost complacent that sin is a serious thing to Jesus. This idea causes me to scratch my head; it makes no sense. Turn to Matthew 4:17 and Luke 13:5, and you will read the words of Christ Himself.

If when Jesus began to preach thought it was important enough to tell those around Him to repent, how can we then say repentance is not important?

There is a time that sin enters all of our lives and we all have a sin that easily besets us (Hebrews 12:1). You know, that sin that we struggle with daily and sometimes by the minute, that we often excuse away, or that we even refuse to acknowledge that it even exists. O taste and see that the Lord is good because God clearly tells us what to do about sin, and there is no need for guessing. He does not want us to have to carry that sin burden around with us.

Devotion 7: The Giver of Eternal Life
Passage: John 10:1-30
Key Verse: John 10:28

As a young child do you remember a time of feeling important because of the person you were with or the person you knew? Maybe it was an adult who let you accompany him or her where children did not normally go, or maybe it was a teacher who always gave you a hall pass whenever you asked. At any rate, it was someone more powerful than you, someone who that gave you entrance to a place you desired.

With that in mind, ask yourself, "Who is Jesus?" One answer could be that He is the gift giver of a free pass to Heaven, the backstage pass, if you will, to the VIP section. In John 10:28, we see that Jesus is the giver of eternal life a great verse to highlight in your Bible if you are the type that marks in their Bible.

It is exciting to know that we can have a *personal relationship* with the One who holds such importance and prominence. I might not know many influential people, but I do know the One who gives eternal life: the God who gave me to Jesus. Think about being loved and held so dear. O taste and see that the Lord is good.

Chapter 2: Devotions 8-14

Devotion 8: Liberal Life-giving Liberation
Passage: John 8:30-36
Key Verse: John 8:36

Perhaps you have seen a movie clip or YouTube clip that shows a young child being put into hand cuffs by a police officer, to scare the child to fly straight. Only to see the child realize it was just a trick as he slips the cuffs off his or her tiny wrists. I love this picture as it reminds me that while sin might have us in a vise grip type hold that drains the very life out of us, we too can smirk and realize there is a way out.

This is where life starts getting victorious for many, when we understand one tiny passage. Turn to John 8:36 and soak it in, I mean *really* soak it in. The Son referred to here is none other than our Lord Jesus Christ. While reading the verse you might ask, free from what? We are free from sin (see John 8:34). Sin has no more dominion or control over you if you are a Christian. Will you sin? Most likely. Must you sin, because you can't help yourself or you are too addicted to the sin of choice? No. The Son gives you liberal life-giving liberation from all sorts of sin bondage. Remember that freedom and liberation the next time you are tempted to sin, because you are not relegated to a life bound by sin, neither am I. So, shake off those cuffs and that bondage to your sin choice because Jesus does give you liberation from it.

O taste and see that the Lord is good as He is the great liberal life-giving liberator. What is your choice? Continue in sin or rest in freedom?

Devotion 9: No Condemnation
Passage: Romans 8:1-2
Key Verse: Romans 8:1

I remember a time in high school that I barely failed an end of year type exam, which prompted my parents to have me take summer school for that subject. Needless to say, I felt like a failure. It was assumed that I needed to pass that exam to get the advanced diploma I was trying to get. At the *end* of the summer school session, we learned that indeed I did not have to retake the test to receive the diploma as I passed the course with no problem. Wow, talk about feeling good about myself again.

Now consider that some of us are told (either implied or directly) they were not a good enough Christian because of sins committed prior to them becoming a Christian. This dear sister is basically told that she is failure and then her struggle begins. She struggles with the label and even starts doubting her own personal standing with God. Not a fun place to be! Why, oh, why do we do this to one another? There is a better way!

Let's turn to Romans 8:1 for help on this very topic. While sin does disqualify one for certain types of service (Titus 1:5–9 and 1 Timothy 3:1–13), it does not condemn the Christian who has confessed and is now living in the Spirit *instead of* the flesh. There is so much to do in a local church that past sin does not permanently disqualify one for, so let's get busy. The real issue is here is this…Does Jesus' blood have the power to forgive sins or not?

His forgiveness covers a multitude of sins for those who are repentant. Has the Lord forgiven you? Then act like He has and enjoy your new life free from condemnation from Him! O taste and see that the Lord is good.

Devotion 10: Jesus the Willing Forgiver
Passage: John 8:1-11
Key Verse: John 8:11

This portion of Scripture deals with the woman caught in adultery. She was about to be stoned to death, even though Old Testament law called for both the man and woman to be stoned and it is so very interesting how the Scribes and Pharisees conveniently "forgot" to bring the man who was caught in adultery with her or she just happened to be in their path and seized the opportunity to grab her (and not search for him) and make a mockery of her to Jesus. The Scribes and Pharisees placed her in the front of them and Jesus for the purpose of attempting to trap Jesus with a question about the laws (talk about messing with someone's life for your personal gain).

They inquired of Jesus if they should stone her based on the Law of Moses. If it is not already interesting to you how they could risk someone's life, it is about to get even more interesting. Jesus basically invites one of them to stone her, that is the one without sin (He already knew the answer).

An amazing thing happens next…all the accusers left, and she was left there alone with Jesus; the sinless God-man. She was left standing next to the One who could stone her, but look at the exciting words of Christ in John 8:10–11.

Did you catch what the Master did? He forgave her and did not give her the death sentence, rather He told her to go on with her life and *sin no more*. I sometimes wonder how our lives would be after we seek forgiveness if we would just go and sin no more. Please note that Jesus is not the accuser, that is Satan (see Revelation 12:10).

The Lord is good, He is the restorer of life, and wants us to live a redeemed life not a life of condemnation. Have you accepted His offer to go and sin no more? If you have not, may I encourage you to?

Devotion 11: Need Rest?

Passage: Matthew 11:28-30
Key Verse: Matthew 11:30

Are you so busy that there is not five minutes to spare in your day? Not even time to sit down for a second? Does everyone expect something of you? Are your own goals a little lofty? Are you burning the candle at both ends, as the saying goes? I have a solution for you. Well, not me, but Jesus does.

Turn to Matthew 11:28–30. Jesus speaks of His yoke being easy; just *learn about Him*. Why not trade your yoke for Jesus' yoke and find rest? Spend some time learning about your Lord, it will be restful. O taste and see that the Lord is good for He is not a burdensome taskmaster, rather the Master who gives rest for our souls. Have you found that sweet rest?

Devotion 12: God's Protection

Passage: Genesis 18:20-19:30
Key Verse: Genesis 19:10

I get the warm fuzzies when I think of God's protection of the righteous ones. I can face tomorrow because I know He protects us, no matter what evil is around us or what circumstances have captured our eyes. Have you ever intended to help someone, and in reality it is they who helped you? I can think of a time when I became a teacher of children to help them, only to learn that they are the ones who ended up teaching and blessing me. In the example that follows we will see that Lot intended to help his guest, only to be helped and protected by them.

In the Old Testament there is the record of the cities and people of Sodom and Gomorrah. In Genesis 18:20-32 we see Abraham interceding for Sodom so that the Lord would not destroy the city if he found 10 righteous people.

As we know, God did not find 10 righteous people in the city of Sodom and He did not save the cities of Sodom or Gomorrah (Genesis 19:24). He did save four people; however, from the city that He was about to destroy (Genesis 19:16). Lot had taken guests into his home trying to protect them, but ultimately these guests are those that saved Lot (Genesis 19:9c–11).

Did you catch what happened? The townspeople were about to hurt Lot's guests but the hand of the guests (the angels) saved Lot and his household. Those meaning to do evil were blinded and could not even find the door. Talk about protection in a mighty way!

The Lord is good. He is the able and willing protector.

Are you doing what is right and leaving the protection up to your Heavenly Father? O taste and see that He is truly good.

Devotion 13: Calmness
Passage: Psalm 23
Key Verse: Psalm 23:2

Life sometimes gets hectic between chores, family, friends, volunteerism, schedules, commutes, social media, commitments, a side hustle, sports, relationships, laundry, church functions, employment, childcare, and the list never seems to end. Sometimes I question, "When is this going to stop so I can take a breather?" Then, once again, the very Word of God is the restorer of my soul. Psalm 23:2 gives us all we need to know.

O, how great those green pastures are. But that is not what grabs me about this verse, it is three other words... *"He makes me"*. Looking back, I can see when life got rough God made me lie down in calm places. It might have been my bedroom, a friend's house, a parent's house, it might have been somewhere else. One thing is sure...I did not lack anything, nor did I lack green pastures and still waters because He led me and made me. Even more interesting is that since He is the creator of everything, He also created and made that green pasture for me and for you. He makes me to lie down by provision and sometimes by force. Let there be no doubt though, He knows exactly when you and I need those green pastures that He already created for us.

O taste and see that the Lord is good, the giver of calmness. Are you fighting the green pastures and calm waters where the Lord is making you go? Do not fight it, sister; accept His guidance and find all the peace you have longed for.

Devotion 14: God Knows the Answer
Passage: Daniel 2
Key Verse: Daniel 2:19

Am I the only one who has had sleepless nights rolling and tossing from one side to another not knowing what the answer was that I desperately needed? I do not think I am alone here. If I were, why are there so many sleep aid commercials? The great thing about the Christian walk is that it does not have to be this way, but if you are like me you have been hard headed before you learned your lesson.

When the answer you are seeking is hard, difficult, allusive, or downright impossible…turn to God. Daniel had an impossible task before him. Daniel's task was to figure out the king's dream and interpret it when the king did not even know the dream himself. Talk about a difficult task. All King Nebuchadnezzar knew was that it was a troubling dream. It was so troubling he was willing to kill his wise men if they did not tell him the dream or its interpretation. Talk about being in a pickle!

This Biblical account is found in Daniel 2. What I find interesting is that Daniel, who was among the wise men of the king's court, was not even asked to interpret the king's dream. You can see in Daniel 2:14, that Daniel heard about the decree rather than being personally summoned by the king. Not only did he hear the decree, but he answered it, knowing full well the possibility of death. Ever find yourself in a situation for which you will suffer consequences if you do not step up and take care of someone else's mess? This is precisely where Daniel found himself.

He surrounds himself with some faith family and employs them to pray to God for the answer (verses 16–18). Notice, he did not consult the king's books, nor what the current gossip was about the king dealings, or who the enemies of the king were. Daniel asks his friends to pray to God for the answer. This is profound! Daniel took an atypical route to solving the problem.

In many places you might very well be scorned for solving a problem in this manner, yet this is how intentionally Daniel approached the problem. Daniel prayed and asked his friends to do likewise. I am thankful for praying friends and I am sure Daniel was too.

By verse 19 we see God honored their request and gave Daniel the answer in a night vision. The rest is history: the wise men were all saved from the king's anger and the king got to know that the God of Abraham, Isaac, and Jacob was indeed the one true God. God wants to show Himself strong in the affairs of His followers so that He *alone* gets the glory. God seems to delight in solving the "unsolvable" for us so that we see Him in all of His glory.

O taste and see that the Lord is good. He is the provider of the answers to all our difficult circumstances and situations. Have you and your friends asked God for an answer? Try Him. You will be amazed by His answers.

Chapter 3: Devotions 15-21

Devotion 15: Fruitful Checklist
Passage: Mark 4
Key Verse: Mark 4:19

Ever become unfruitful and wonder why? Why am I not successfully showing God's love? Why am I not witnessing? Why is my anger out of control? Jesus gave us an incredibly easy three-point checklist to help us identify the problem and it does not even require an appointment with the pastor, the Sunday School teacher, or even a small group leader for that matter.

Turn to Mark 4:19 with me. Jesus Himself told us that there are three things that make the Word of God unfruitful in our lives: (1) the cares of the world, (2) deceitfulness of riches, and (3) lust of other things. This is a simple list, not a long list of character traits or even a family lineage. Is something keeping you from being fruitful in your Christian walk? If there is, it is probably one of the above-mentioned reasons. Let's address root causes and not just symptoms.

God is the God of simplicity. Let's keep it simple, stop all the sleepless nights, and address the real problems (of which there are only three options). O taste and see that the Lord is good. We do not serve a God who makes things impossible for us or gives us everything in a riddle; our God is straightforward.

Devotion 16: Love

Passage: Genesis 29
Key Verse: Genesis 29:20

In reading Genesis 29 I was struck about this idea of love, that love is more than just an emotion or a warm fuzzy feeling. Everyone likes those feelings, right? I mean Hollywood and Hallmark sell a lot of television time because we love warm, fuzzy, love stories.

What about a love that is defined by an action? There is an example of this in Genesis 29 where we read that Jacob loved Rachel (verse 18) and was willing to work seven years for her (verse 20), and in reality ended up working fourteen years for her (verse 20, 27, and 30). How different things are in our world today! Jacob was willing, and in fact did, work fourteen years (verse 20 and 27–28) for the object of his love. Many today do not even stay married for seven years.

What if a young man had to work for his future father-in-law to win the hand of the one he loved in marriage? What if he showed his love by working instead of playing all day long? How long would he work: an hour, a day, a week, a month? O taste and see that the Lord is good! He gave us a glimpse of true love... a love that endures.

Devotion 17: No Guess Work

Passage: Proverbs 6:15-19
Key Verse: Proverbs 6:16

Ever wonder what someone likes and does not like? It is kind of like a guessing game and you end up just hoping you get it right. This actually happens daily in the lives of many people. Ever wish someone would just shoot straight with you so you did not have to guess? Ever wish that parent or boss would just tell you what they wanted and did not want so you could just hop to it instead of guessing?

Hop on over to Proverbs 6:16–19. God is very clear about seven things that He does not like. No more guessing games; it is simple, straight forward, and not complicated at all.

God does not make us guess what He does not like. His Word shares with us everything we need to know! Do you know what God likes and doesn't like?

Devotion 18: Names

Passage: Exodus 6:13-26
Key Verse: Exodus 6:20

Have you ever noticed that individual names are mentioned a lot in the Holy Scriptures? Not just family names, but individual names as well. I have always referred to the mother of Moses as "The mother of Moses." I am also guilty of doing this in everyday life. How about you? Have you ever said, "I saw Judy's daughter," or "Was that Chuck's daughter"?

Then I was reminded in the Scriptures that even Moses's mother has a name and it is Jochebed. This is recorded for us in Exodus 6:20, and her relationship to Moses and Aaron is restated in verse 26. Individuals matter to God and I pray individuals also matter to us.

O taste and see that the Lord is good, because individuals matter, not just our position or relationship to another. Our God is a personal God. You matter to God and so do I.

Devotion 19: The Favor Grantor

Passage: Daniel 1:5-15
Key Verse: Daniel 1:9

It is nice to be found in favor with someone, especially with the ones you love and adore. As children we have longed to be the favored one and as Christians we are favored! What's more is that we need to remember where this favor comes from.

Let's take a peek at Daniel 1:9. Please do not skip reading this little verse, actually get your Bible out and read it. It clearly shows that it was God who brought Daniel into favor and tender love with the prince of the eunuchs. God brought Daniel into favor with those around him. Having trouble with those around you? A good place to start would be to pray to the Giver of favor and ask Him to grant you favor with those around you.

The Lord wants to grant you favor for His divine purposes. He has done it in the past for others and wants to do it for you as well. O taste and see that the Lord is good.

Devotion 20: The Tempter Answered

Passage: Matthew 4:1-11
Key Verse: Mathew 4:10

Are we prepared to handle temptations? One way to find out is to look at the Scriptures you have memorized. For some, John 3:16 is the first verse they ever memorized as a child, and as an adult is the only verse they can recite. Yet others can quote many verses but cannot tell you where they are found in the Bible. Then there are the few who seem to be a walking Bible because of their memorization of Scripture.

Matthew 4:3-4, 7, 10 recall for us the earthly temptation of Jesus and how He personally handled it. This might be a great Scripture to highlight in your Bible so it can be easily found again. Jesus answered the tempter with the very words of God, quoting from Scripture, and notice, He did not quote a chapter and verse, He simply quoted Scripture.

How much Scripture do you have available for when the tempter strikes? Remember, you do not have to have chapter and verse to quote the text, you only need it to find the text if you do not have a Bible app on your phone or an internet connection to search for it.

O taste and see that the Lord is good for He gave us the way to deal with the tempter if we would avail ourselves of it. May I challenge you to memorize some Scripture?

Devotion 21: Identity Securer

Passage: Acts 27:13-25
Key Verses: Acts 27:22-23

I remember a time growing up when my grandfather had remarried long after the death of my maternal grandmother. This remarriage included adding another uncle to the family who was about my own age. As you can imagine there was some jealousy and vying for positions of control and influence. I recall a time when I was threatened by this young uncle, saying that he could kill me (literally). I remember saying to him something to the effect of "Go ahead and kill me, and when I am dead Grandpa will kill you." I was confident in my identity as Grandpa's grandchild, almost felt like a child of the king who was untouchable. By the way, we got along fine after that episode and lived to tell stories about it.

When we know our identity we can face uncertain times and circumstances. Paul did just that and a gracious God made sure it was recorded for our enrichment. Acts 27:23 is a very interesting read in the Scriptures. Paul was in the middle of a personal storm and yet he was calm. Why? Because he knew who he was, who he belonged to, and the promises God made to him. So, who do you belong to? Who are you? Your calmness and happiness are directly tied to your identity not the circumstances in which you find yourself. Does your identity need a tune up?

O taste and see that the Lord is good. He has given each of us ladies an identity and a purpose.

Chapter 4: Devotions: 22-28

Devotion 22: Favorite Verses
Passage: Genesis 20
Key Verse: Genesis 20:18

It is intriguing to me what people tell me their favorite verse or life verse is. More intriguing is the verse or verses that people cling to during certain seasons of their life. Growing up, as a young child, I clung to Matthew 5:43–48, as it spoke to how I should handle myself when being constantly picked on.

As I went through what I affectionately call my "wilderness wandering," it was comforting to cling to Genesis 12:17 and 20:18. Scripture records that God did things for the benefit of a specific woman named Sarah. God did some things "because of." To know that our God is not a God who elevates men at the cost of women. No, He is a God who cares about women as well.

There seems to be a verse for every season of life in which you might find yourself. When you find a verse that speaks volumes to you take note, copy it, circle it, highlight it, whatever it takes to help you to remember it and cling to it.

I so want to continue to taste and see that the Lord is good and I also want to taste and see what God does on my behalf. What about you?

Devotion 23: Our God Cares
Passage: 1 Peter 5:5-10
Key Verse: 1 Peter 5:7

In Christian circles it almost goes without saying that God cares. We often recite the familiar verse: 1 Peter 5:7. There are two words that I would like to focus on for this verse…casting and all. Yes, we know that God cares, but do we cast or give *ALL* our cares to Him? Do we really give them to the Lord and leave them there? Or do we, more accurately, give Him some of our cares and carry the rest of them by ourselves? Or do we give them to Him only to find ourselves taking them back the next day.

God is the all-knowing one who can really *do* something about all of our cares and worries. He just wants us to give them to Him.

O taste and see that the Lord is good, and that He *really* does care for you and me.

Devotion 24: God is Faithful

Passage: 1 Corinthians 10:1-14
Key Verse: 1 Corinthians 10:13

Have you ever read the many promises God makes to us? There is one specifically that grabs my attention; it is found in 1 Corinthians 10:13. It really is worth the read. In the past and at the time of the writing of this book, I stand amazed at the times God is so *faithful* to a sinner like me, to provide yet another way of escape. Jesus was tempted yet without sin, and is fully capable of helping (succor) you and me (Hebrews 2:18). Ever feel like you can't beat a temptation? Jesus is ready to help. Is your temptation or enticing sin attempting to whip your back side?

He is faithful to provide you and me with a means of escape in the midst of temptation if only we would seek Him for the escape route. He already has it mapped out for us. O taste and see that there truly is a way out, if we but seek and ask God for the answer.

Devotion 25: Children Matter to God

Passage: Genesis 21:14-17
Key Verse: Genesis 21:17

My children have asked me, "Does God hear my prayers?" To which I replied with a hearty… "of course He does." The best part is that it is not just words I am saying. These words are backed by the powerful words of Scripture.

In this passage we see Hagar voicing that she does not want to witness the death of her child, in fact she is weeping over what she thinks is to be the near and unavoidable death of her child. It is in this time of desperation that things get exciting. An angel of God responds to her and tells her that God heard the voice of her *child*. Scripture does not say that her voice was heard but the voice of the lad.

If that is not convincing enough, that God cares about children, look no further than Matthew 19:13-15. Jesus cares enough to make sure the children are prayed for and not turned away.

Plain and simple, children matter to God. O taste and see that some of the most vulnerable among us are cared for!

Devotion 26: Debt Reliever
Passage: 1 John 4
Key Verse: 1 John 4:10

Jesus brought to us the good will of the Father by paying a debt for us that we could not pay for ourselves. As we all know, our actions or lack of action have consequences. When we sin there are consequences. Consequences can be small or large in our lives here on earth, but make no mistake the consequence for sin is an eternal one called death (Romans 6:23).

The good news is found in a New Testament verse (1 John 4:10) and it relays this concept quite nicely. Jesus is our propitiation or the One who appeases or pays the Father on our behalf. Jesus pays the debt we cannot pay. Is it not wonderful to be relieved of debt and all the worrisome days and nights it brings?

If your sin debt has not been paid, please talk with a trusted Christian friend or pastor, or contact whetonline.com for more guidance.

Devotion 27: Trouble Lifter
Passage: Psalm 34
Key Verse: Psalm 34:6

We have heard that David was a man after God's own heart (Acts 13:22), yet even he needed to be rescued. Being loved by God does not mean we will have no troubles, just take a look at the life of David. David was in circumstances that compelled him to cry out to the Lord.

Better than just being heard by God, he was saved from *all* of his troubles (Psalms 34:6). Can you give testimony to someone else that the Lord saved you out of your troubles? Or, like David, are you in a place where you need to cry out?

Either way, O taste and see that the Lord is good for He hears *and* delivers us from troubles, if we will just cry out to Him. He wants to be strong on our behalf.

Devotion 28: God the Pace Setter

Passage: Matthew 5:43-48
Key Verse: Matthew 5:45

Have you ever met others different from you? You know, they wear their hair different, they talk funny, they walk different, you know, just plain different. I have. I have come to love these different ones. I see something special in each of them. Okay, they are different, but they are nonetheless precious.

I have loved one with bold pink hair after she had the opportunity to tell me of the origins of her pink hair. The story showed her courage and the will of a momma to protect her children and see them to safety. I got to see a piece of her beautiful soul.

Acts 10:34b shows us that our God does not play favorites, and Matthew 5:45b shows us that He sends the sun and rain to everyone. He sends it to all regardless of how they treat Him, regardless if they are like us or not.

God sets the pace for kind acts. He is kind to all, even when it is not deserved or earned. Have you showed *His* kind of kindness today even to those who are different from you (like someone with pink hair or maybe a tattoo)? Will you allow your kindness or goodness to fall on the different ones? O taste and see that the Lord is good. He sends the rain to us, regardless of who we are.

Chapter 5: Devotions 29-35

Devotion 29: Word Power
Passage: Nehemiah 8:5-12
Key Verse: Nehemiah 8:9

I entered the building full of excitement and expectation. Others came and likewise were exuberant. All intently listened, not wanting to miss a single note or word. Sounds like people were going to a concert, doesn't it? The truth is we were attending a worship service. Have you ever gone to a church in that kind of mode, excited and wondering what was going to be read from the Scriptures?

The people of Israel did. Nehemiah shares the humbling account of Ezra opening the book and reading to the people while they *stood* and causing them to understand the law of the Lord, so much so that they began to weep!

No complaining of how long the service took, that their feet hurt, that they were hungry, the loudness or softness of the music, the chosen topic, the color of the walls, the darkness or lightness of the sanctuary walls, the plushness of the seats or lack thereof, or anything like that. Wow, talk about a revival service.

The power of God's word is not limited to the time of Ezra. Isaiah 55:11 gives us a reminder of the fact that God's word goes from God's mouth and does not return void. Thank you, God, for preserving your word for us in the Holy Scriptures that we too can join in on the power of your word with excitement and anticipation. O taste and see that the Lord is good.

Devotion 30: Good Gifts
Passage: Matthew 7: 1-11
Key Verse: Matthew 7:11

Ever see others receiving good gifts from God and wonder why it seems as though you are not receiving good gifts from God? I have and, thankfully, God through His word taught me a valuable lesson.

The first is in James 1:17, which tells us that our God *is* the giver of good gifts. But then, why was everyone but me receiving good gifts from God? I would learn soon enough the reason was not that God is not a good gift giver to me, but rather I was not doing my part.

Take a peek, if you will, at Matthew 7:11. Did you catch what the Scripture says? Our Heavenly Father gives good gifts to those of His children who *ask* Him. I had not asked Him; but I have since learned to ask Him for many different good things (as defined by God). This does not mean He always gives us everything we want.

O taste and see that the Lord is good. He truly is the good gift giver and delights in our asking in accordance to His will.

Devotion 31: The Prepper
Passage: Mark 13:20-33
Key Verse: Mark 13:23

O taste and see that the Lord is good. He has not left us with no knowledge of the end times or the false prophets that will rise. The end times do not have to be a scary thing for us, nor do we have to wonder if we will fall for the false christs. The Lord has already revealed to us all we need to know.

In Mark 13:20–33, the good Lord reminds us that He has foretold how the end times are going to be, so that we need not be tricked by anyone.

O taste and see that the Lord is good. He has prepped us for the days ahead. No need to worry, read His word and get prepped up!

Devotion 32: Dress Your Faith Up

Passage: James 2:14-19
Key Verse: James 2:18

Ever get yourself in a quandary about what others might think of you wearing a particular outfit? Admit it, ladies, you know what I am talking about. Should I wear the red top with this pair of jeans or the purple one? Do I look thinner with the red one, more professional with the purple one? The list goes on and on. It seems that what we put on says a lot about who we are and if we value ourselves or not. It just might be the same when it comes to or faith.

Jump over to James 2:18 and read it carefully, twice if need be. It appears to me that our works become the clothes by which others can see our faith. Remember, people can't see your faith, but they can see the result of your faith.

The next time you assess your attire in the mirror, remember to assess how your faith is looking. What are your works showing?

Devotion 33: A Lot of Faith

Passage: Matthew 17:14-21
Key Verse: Matthew 17:20

I used to ask The Lord to give me a lot of faith, big faith, just a good measure of the stuff. You know, shaken down and patted down like you would if making cookies with brown sugar. That is how I wanted the Lord to measure out faith to me, measured, pressed down and measured again.

Then, I read Matthew 17:20 with a new set of eyes. It was like I was reading it for the first time. Have a try at it; and take a moment to read it. It seems that a dash of faith (instead of a well-pressed cup) did some amazing things. Some mustard seeds are a mere two mm in size, yet produce the large mustard plant. Perfectly sized faith moves mountains, obstacles, and others.

What in the world would a large faith do, say the size of a peach seed? Lord, please just give us that little faith you spoke to your disciples about. I desire that tiny faith that is *so* mighty, because I don't think I am ready for a cupful.

Devotion 34: Belief and Fear
Passage: Mark 5:20-43
Key Verse: Mark 5:36

In your mind's eye will you picture with me a relaxing pool on a perfect summer's day with a gentle breeze? Now, place a young child at the pool's edge with a parent in the water with their arms spread out and upwards towards the child. Can you hear the conversation? The parent lovingly saying: "You trust me, right? Don't be afraid, just jump, I will catch you." Now, depending upon how much fear or faith in the parent your imagined child has, they either jump or cling to the side of the pool like there is no hope for tomorrow.

Mark 5:36 is the spiritual equivalent of this scenario. Jesus tells a father not to fear, only believe. It seems as though fear of this type has no place in faith and believing. Fear becomes a barometer, if you will, showing us where our faith is. Is our faith gone or strong?

O taste and see that the Lord is good. He gave us a belief that can triumph over fear.

Devotion 35: Faith's Doing Power
Passage: Hebrews 11
Key Verse: Hebrews 11:33+

Has your focus ever been off? I know mine has been. For instance, I remember when I was told a riddle and could not figure it out, only to realize later that the reason I could not solve it is because I was focused on the wrong part of the riddle. Once my focus was right, the riddle was *ultra-simple*.

Hebrews 11 is known as the Hall of Faith, a list of heroes of the faith, if you will. For many years, every time I read this passage I would focus on all these people with incredible faith, missing a major point altogether because my focus was one-sided.

Changing my focus from the people to faith makes this passage come alive. Can't believe I missed it for so long. Go ahead read Hebrews 11 again with a new focus.

Did you come up with what I came up with? Faith gives intellect to the beginning of the world, caused the offering of an excellent sacrifice, made one not experience death, makes possible to please God, makes people heirs of righteousness, causes obedience, and is an agent of conception.

I see in God's word faith doing many things and causing many things. It makes me wonder what my faith is doing and causing? The faith that is doing nothing is dead (James 2:26), so what is your faith doing?

O taste and see that the Lord is good. While it is important to see what people did because of faith, it is also awesome to see what faith is capable of.

Chapter 6: Devotions 36-42

Devotion 36: Belief to Do
Passage: Matthew 14:22-34
Key Verse: Matthew 14:31

Have you begun to do something you know you were told by God to do, then something hinders your ability to do it and you start to sink? Then you doubt that God even told you to do it in the first place, because, after all, if God told you to do it you should be able to do it and not be sinking. Can you relate?

Matthew 14:22-32 shows us that we can relate to Peter, who also would have related to us if he was still living. Peter had a directive to go to the other side and was hindered by a storm.

This is where I have errored in the past. I, like Peter, was told to do something...so I tried to do it in my own strength. But that is where the problem lies. I tried instead of relying on the One who lives within me. Then something came along to hinder my ability to finish the task, and I am reminded that God sent me to do a task *and* I need His help to finish the task.

In verse 31 Jesus stretches His hand to save Peter and says, "O thou of little faith, wherefore didst thou doubt?" Oh, that statement stings! Jesus basically is saying, "I told you to do something, do you not think I would make sure you could finish it?" After all, Jesus was not asking Peter to do anything he was capable of doing all by himself.

Has He told you something? Then know that regardless of what happens He will see you through to the completion of the task, and that, my sister, is what I call a prescription for success with no worries! This is because it is not about you or about me, but about the One who does the calling.

Devotion 37: Help My Unbelief
Passage: Mark 9
Key Verse: Mark 9:24

Have you come to a place in your life where you believe in the Lord Jesus Christ as your Lord and Savior? (I sincerely hope so.) Then life continues and you come to a place where you know God wants to do something, but you do not know what and you certainly do not know why God would use you for such a task. I have been there and will be there again. Mark 9 speaks to my heart during times like these.

We see a father who did not give up on finding help for his son who was possessed of a foul spirit. He came to Jesus and asked help for his son. Jesus tells the father in verse 23 that all things are possible to the person who believes. I find the father's response in verse 24 most interesting. Go ahead and quickly read it.

My mind was blown. The father believed and yet he had unbelief. Talk about transparency with his Lord. He recognized that he believed, but still needed help to believe more. Oh, that salvation would not be the stopping place for us, but rather be just the *starting* place for us to grow.

When God has you in a place to do something big and you are at the point of doubting...cry out, "Lord, I believe, please help me in my unbelief," then taste and see that He is faithful to help with your unbelief.

Devotion 38: Faith or Sight
Passage: Hebrews 11
Key Verse: Hebrews 11:7

I think at times my eyes allow me to have more grief than I need. This is because my eyes look at the circumstances around me and take it all in. The eye sees the rolling eyes of others, the eye sees injustices, the eye sees misunderstandings, and the list seems never to end. Have you been there?

Then, I am reminded that as Christians we live by faith and not by sight (II Corinthians 5:7). Noah gives us an example of living by faith. By faith he built an ark that seemed unnecessary (for it had not rained on the earth yet). Can you imagine making a huge boat for an event that had never happened before? This is what Hebrews 11:7 shares with us. Noah's actions were determined by his faith not his sight. Does faith or sight move you to action? O taste and see that the Lord is good and has provided a faith is mightier than sight.

Devotion 39: Walking by Sight

Passage: II Corinthians 4:3-18
Key Verse: II Corinthians 4:18

I do not know about you, but I certainly walk by sight sometimes. Your child breaks a bone, you have several appointments in one day (each at other ends of the world it seems), and you have commitments to last you all week. Sound familiar? At those times my sight is on earthly things, until a sister or brother brings the Light of the Lord back to me. I received one such email. This email reminded me that the schedule I keep has a purpose.

That purpose is to effect people for an eternal purpose. I was thankful for the gratitude expressed in the email and was reminded that I do what I do simply so another can be touched by the love of God.

How is your focus today, have you lived by sight with a focus on temporal things or have you lived by faith with a focus on eternal things? II Corinthians 4:18 should be reread and oft shared with others to help keep us focused.

Devotion 40: Love
Passage: Galatians 5:14-15
Key Verse: Galatians 5:15

Our walk is very simple if done God's way. Turn with me to Galatians 5:14-15.

Why do Christians have such a difficult time with this one? Love others or be consumed by one another. Our faith and walk are simple; let's do it together. We have been given the greatest love anyone was ever given. God loved, God gave Jesus, Jesus lived a perfect sinless life, shed His blood for us to rise again into life eternal to offer you and me total forgiveness. This is the love we have to offer and treat each other with.

Are you already consumed by broken relationships, anger, bitterness, pride, etc.? There is hope. Start by loving and forgiving. That is exactly what the greatest love did for us. God loved and forgave us through the blood of Christ. If you will begin to love and forgive, you will be amazed what God can do through you.

The choice is mine and the choice is yours: love or be consumed. O taste and see that the Lord is good. He gives a love that can bind us together instead of tearing us apart.

Devotion 41: Bringing Scriptures to Life
Passage: John 21:1-17
Key Verse: John 21:17

Sometimes I like to substitute my name in Bible verse for the names that are there to question or to understand a point a little better. As little kids, some of us were taught John 3:16 by substituting our names for the word "world." This is kind of the same thing I am going to do with the verses for today.

For today's text let's look at the words of Christ in John 21:15-17. Read it first the way it is written, then read it a second time replacing Simon's name with your name and relationship. For me, it then reads "Tanya, daughter of Charles, lovest thou me? Feed my lambs." Now this verse comes to life for me.

You see, I know I can substitute my name in this verse for Simon because Matthew 28:20 commands me and you to teach others of Christ, which is feeding the lambs. The question then becomes do I love Christ enough to feed His lambs? What about you? Do you love enough?

Devotion 42: Love that Gave
Passage: John 3:13-18
Key Verse: John 3:16

I know many people who define love as what others can do for them or by Hollywood's portrayal of sexual intimacy. This saddens me. The Scriptures tell us that God is love (I John 4:8). What is more exciting is that Scripture also gives us a glimpse of what true love is. We read in John 3:16 that God gave. *Love gives*. Love does not demand or say "give me" or "give me now."

As we go day to day are we mindful that many around us do not know that God even gave them a gift? If you have accepted God's gift of love are you hoarding it or sharing that gift with others by loving enough to give? Do you not know about this gift? Read the book of John, the book of Romans, or talk to your Christian friend, pastor, or contact us at whetonline.com.

Chapter 7: Devotions 43-49

Devotion 43: Love that is Sacrificial
Passage: I John 3:13-18
Key Verse: I John 3:16

John 3:16 is very familiar to those of us who grew up in church, but what about I John 3:16? I John 3:16 shows us that the love that God has for us is not one that was cheap, passive, or inactive! Neither should our love for others around us be cheap, passive, or inactive.

It is not an act of love to donate your tattered clothes to those in need or to give of the worst of what you own to others. Love necessitates that we be sacrificial...His life was laid down for us. Did you catch that in the key verse?

What a mouthful!! When was the last time we were inconvenienced for someone other than ourselves? When did we lay something down for someone else? O taste and see that the Lord is good. He was sacrificial for us!

Devotion 44: Longing to be Loved

Passage: Proverbs 8:13-21
Key Verse: Proverbs 8:17

Ever thought "I just want to be loved?" If so, I have some great news for you! Proverbs 8:17 gives us the simple mathematical equation to determine if we are loved by God. Interesting thing: it depends on us, not Him. He is ready, able, and willing to love you! Do you love God?

Notice I did not ask: Do you believe in God? Even the demons believe in God (James 2:19). Here is a two-question Scripture-based quiz to see if you are loved by God:

Quiz question number 1, read Proverbs 8:17. If you are loved by God, you will be rebuked and chastened by Him. Have you been rebuked by God? If you have, then know you are loved! A father does not correct a child he does not love!

Quiz question number 2, find and read two verses: I John 4:20-21. Do you hate your brother? If so, the love of God is not in you.

Do you love God? Does God love you? Sometimes the truth can sting, other times it is reassuring. O taste and see that the Lord is good and will tell you the truth.

Devotion 45: Loved While a Sinner
Passage: Romans 5:1-10
Key Verse: Romans 5:8

My husband's favorite verse for many years has been Romans 5:8. What an amazing thought: Christ died for me when I was a sinner. He did not die for me because I was righteous or all put together. He loved me BEFORE I was loveable.

Many of us have this backwards. In our human relationships we give to those doing right things and kick our wounded or fallen. What about loving sinners and reaching out to them as Christ reached out to us as sinners?

O taste and see that the Lord is good. We do not have to have it all together and be perfect to be loved by Him.

Devotion 46: Forgiveness a High Calling
Passage: Matthew 6:1-21
Key Verse: Matthew 6:14-15

Ever been hurt bad, I mean really bad by a friend, relative, co-worker, or boss? Hurt by one you though would never betray you, by someone you trusted? I think we all have, and if you have not been hurt, hang on, your day is coming because we live in a fallen world.

When hurting, we can deny it happened and kind of ignore it. While hurting we, can become angry, bitter, or spiteful. Often times I hear ladies say, "I can't forgive him/her, I do not feel like forgiving him/her, because it hurts too bad to forgive." Any of this sound familiar?

Jesus showed us a better way. He offered us forgiveness when He hurt bad on that cross. He showed us how to forgive the unlovable. He just did it. He did it because He loved us. Herein is the truth: we can forgive even the greatest offenses if we love one another.

Also, during His ministry here on earth, Jesus gave us another motivator to forgive others. It is found in Matthew 6:14-15, and is a very interesting read. Is it worth holding a grudge and not forgiving someone, when it means you not receiving forgiveness from God? Something to think about.

Devotion 47: Love the Enemy
Passage: Matthew 5
Key Verse: Matthew 5:43-44

My favorite verse growing up was Matthew 5:43-44, which can be a critical verse if you grew up being picked on. Growing up hearing impaired was challenging at times and downright trying at other times. God, however, revealed His plan for me dealing with life's adversaries.

His way kept me from growing up bitter and angry. As an adult, I see many people shackled in anger and bitterness. If we can learn to love our enemies, anger and bitterness cannot control our lives and victory is ours through Jesus Christ.

So, are you loving your enemies? Are you good to those that hate you? Do you pray for your persecutors? Victory in Christ is yours if you will humbly submit to His will in your life, and do it His way. O taste and see that the Lord is good. He gives us the recipe for victory in our lives.

Devotion 48: Worship
Passage: Job 1
Key Verse: Job 1:21

When my oldest was nine years old, her favorite verse was Job 1:21b. In general, we are on cloud nine when God blesses us, but how many of us bless God when blessings are taken away (not just the absence of blessings) from us? When God takes things and loved ones from us, can we bless Him and thereby truly worship Him? Do you bless and worship God regardless of the situation in which you find yourself?

This can be a very difficult thing to do; however, notice Job did not sin saying that God took something from him. Sometimes a true statement (like God took something from you) becomes part of our worship.

O taste and see that the Lord is good. Even the worst times of our lives can be given to the Lord in worship. Hard, yes. Impossible, no.

Devotion 49: Words and Meditation
Passage: Psalm 19:7-14
Key Verse: Psalm 19:14

When my youngest was ten, her favorite verse was Psalm 19:14. This verse reminded her that she should be in a constant habit of pleasing God, because the very words we say all day long should be pleasing to our God.

I wonder how much thought goes into the words we speak. What about when our volume is demeaning? What about when our words are kind and true?

O taste and see that the Lord is good. He even allows us to please Him with our mere words.

ABOUT THE AUTHOR

Tanya Salter is wife to Perry, a bi-vocational pastor, and mom to two incredible young ladies: Hannah and Kelli. As graduate of Liberty University, Tanya holds a Master's Degree in Counseling. She has counseled with people aged three and up, dealing with various topics ranging from depression to major life changes. She left her professional career as a Counselor to raise and home school her two girls, for which she has no regrets.

Additional Devotionals Available at:

whetonline.com

Made in USA - North Chelmsford, MA
1349407_9781729145166
12.28.2022 1143